FASTBACK® Science Fiction

Just in Case

JON NIKISCHER

GLOBE FEARON
Pearson Learning Group

FASTBACK® SCIENCE FICTION BOOKS

The Champion	In the Zone
Dateline: I.P.S.	**Just in Case**
Eden's Daughters	Sinking Ship
The Flavorist	The Spotter
Hennesy's Test	Vital Force

Cover © Royalty-Free/Corbis. All photography © Pearson Education, Inc. (PEI) unless specifically noted.

Copyright © 2004 by Pearson Education, Inc., publishing as Globe Fearon®, an imprint of Pearson Learning Group, 299 Jefferson Road, Parsippany, NJ 07054. All rights reserved. No part of this book may be reproduced or transmitted in any form or by any means, electronic or mechanical, including photocopying, recording, or by any information storage and retrieval system, without permission in writing from the publisher. For information regarding permission(s), write to Rights and Permissions Department.

Globe Fearon® and Fastback® are registered trademarks of Globe Fearon, Inc.

ISBN 0-13-024578-X
Printed in the United States of America
1 2 3 4 5 6 7 8 9 10   07 06 05 04 03

Pearson Learning Group

1-800-321-3106
www.pearsonlearning.com

My name is Hector Luz. I'm writing this while the facts are clear in my mind. I figure it's a good idea to get it down on paper—just in case.

Andrew Garrett was always different from the rest of us. For one thing, he didn't have a family of his own. He stayed with the Porters. They weren't his real parents, and he hadn't been adopted, either. He lived with them as part of their huge family. They were his foster parents. The county paid them something every month for taking care of him.

Andy was in the same seventh-grade class I was placed in. He was so ordinary he was unusual. I saw it the first day. That was the first time I saw him, and I guess I was the only one who noticed it. There didn't seem to be a single thing to set him apart from the rest of us. That seemed odd to me.

We all have things that make us different from each other. But not Andy. He was of average height and weight. His hair was a neutral brown. His voice wasn't distinctive, and he was no noisier or quieter than anyone else.

Andy was a fair student. He tried to avoid being called on in class, and he sometimes gave the wrong answer.

It was years before I realized how very different Andy might be. It happened the summer after our junior year of high school. We went to Arrow Lake one Saturday. Bobby Petersen had the use of his brother's car.

I remember the three of us were strolling along the shore with our hands in our pockets. We were trying to look as though we didn't see the three young women nearby. They were having a picnic. Bobby and I were talking loudly and laughing. We wanted them to notice us.

Andy was so busy looking at one of them that he didn't see a tree root that was sticking out of the ground. He tripped over it and fell forward. His hands had been deep in his pockets. There was a good chance he'd smash his face on a rock or something. But he didn't. As he fell, he somehow got his hands in front of him to break his fall. He ended up looking as if he were about to do push-ups.

When he scrambled to his feet, I saw that his jeans were torn badly. He had pulled his hands from his pockets with such force that he'd ripped the heavy denim.

That cloth was thick and strong. The pockets were reinforced with extra stitching and rivets at the corners. Andy had torn them as easily as he would have torn tissue paper.

Bobby and I were so surprised that all we could do was shake our heads. "You certainly were lucky," said Bobby.

"I thought you were going to get hurt," I said. "How did you get your hands out of your pockets so fast?"

Andy looked at his torn pants with a puzzled expression.

Suddenly a female voice said, "I read that people sometimes do incredible things when they're scared. A woman once lifted a car to save her husband, who was pinned under it in an accident."

"I heard that, too," Bobby said. Perhaps he had. Bobby never liked to admit that anyone knew something he didn't.

Andy, Bobby, and I then introduced ourselves to Susan, Elaine, and Mary.

Andy and Mary hit it off right away. They sat apart from us talking quietly. It was like a meeting between long-lost friends. I'd never seen Andy with so much to talk about. He was usually shy.

I mentioned this, and Susan and Elaine laughed. "We could say the same thing about Mary," Elaine said. "She almost never talks."

Bobby and I saw Susan and Elaine a couple of times after that day. Then, as happens, we met other people, they met other people, and that was the end of it.

Andy and Mary, on the other hand, were almost inseparable. They went to dances and to football and basketball games together. We seldom saw one without the other.

I thought it was great. I mean, Andy was so plain and ordinary. If he hadn't met Mary, he never would have had a date in high school. There was nothing about him that would catch anyone's attention.

Mary, by the way, was also like that. I was amazed at how easily she avoided being noticed.

During our last year of high school, something else happened. One Friday afternoon, there was a baseball game on the diamond behind the school. Baseball wasn't the big deal that basketball and football were. Hardly any of the guys brought dates. Andy came with Bobby and me and sat with us in the bleachers.

It was one of the first games of the season and was very boring. Most of our good players from the last year had graduated. We didn't know any of the visiting players. There's nothing worse than watching a ball game when you don't know the players. You don't know what to expect from them or when to be disappointed.

At the end of the sixth inning, the visiting team was ahead by ten runs. That didn't make things very interesting either. We all decided to leave early. Bobby had his brother's car with him, as he usually did. We wanted to beat the crowd out of the parking lot.

Bobby and Andy got up, but I remained seated. I wanted to see how the batter would do. He was a tall guy with heavy shoulders. He looked as if he could send a ball to the moon if he could get some wood on it.

Get this picture clear in your mind so you can appreciate what happened next: I was sitting in the tenth row of the bleachers, halfway between home plate and first base. Andy and Bobby were standing in front of me with their backs to the batter.

Just as Bobby was about to ask me why I wasn't getting up to leave, the pitcher decided to give the crowd a look at his fastball. It came whistling toward the plate as if it had come from a cannon up the pitcher's sleeve.

The batter must have liked them high and outside; he leaned forward, trying to connect with it. He fouled it back with just enough arc to clear the backstop. It came rocketing at the back of Andy's head in a blur of spin and speed.

But, fast as the ball was traveling, Andy Garrett was faster. He made a half turn to the left, brought up his left arm, and caught the ball with one hand.

There hadn't been an inch of wasted motion. It had seemed casual, almost lazy. Everyone who saw it roared approval. That catch was something to cheer about after the long boring game.

I was watching Andy's face. He didn't look at all happy or excited. He looked worried. He looked as though he'd made a mistake and was wondering how to correct it.

Then he did a surprising thing. He opened his fingers and let the ball fall. He didn't have to drop it; he did it on purpose. He wanted to lessen the shock of what he'd done. I was sure of it.

The crowd groaned.

Bobby finally realized what had happened. "How did you do that?" he asked.

Andy acted confused. It was the same way he had acted the day he had torn his heavy denim jeans. "I'm not sure," he said. "I saw something out of the corner of my eye and put my hand up. Next thing I knew, the ball hit it."

That satisfied Bobby, but I didn't believe it for a second. To see that ball coming he'd have had to have eyes in the back of his head.

I didn't say anything. I just looked at Andy, seeing him differently than I ever had before.

We walked out to the parking lot. While Bobby ran to get the car, Andy turned to me. "You think you just saw me do something weird, don't you?" he asked seriously.

I shrugged. "Not weird. Strange, maybe. Unusual."

"But you don't think it happened the way I said, do you?" His level blue eyes were boring into me.

"No, I don't."

"Are you my friend?" he asked.

"Sure, I am," I said.

"Then do me a favor. Don't talk about this to anyone. Let's pretend it never happened."

I could tell this was important to him. "Let's pretend *what* never happened?" I asked.

He smiled, understanding me perfectly, as he always did. Then Bobby pulled up and we raced for the car.

We never did mention the incident again, but I thought about it a lot. And I began to watch Andy very, very carefully. And I began to wonder.

I wondered why a guy as quick and strong as Andy never went out for any of the teams. I wondered why he could explain math and science to me but never got high grades himself. I wondered why he never volunteered an answer in class.

Andy and I usually walked home from school together. One day I asked him, "How come you try so hard to be average? How come you don't like to be noticed?"

At first I thought he would just smile and shrug. That's what he usually did when anyone asked him a personal question. This time he didn't smile.

He paused, searching for the right words. "Well," he said slowly, "I guess you could say I'm careful."

"Careful?"

"Or maybe I just want people to like me."

I didn't say anything, so he explained: "Humans don't like anyone who is different. It doesn't always make much sense, but that's the way it is. All through history people who were different have had it tough. Some became targets. If you stand out from the others, there's always someone who will hate you or be jealous."

"For example?"

"Minorities everywhere in the world, and individuals like the Kennedy brothers, Martin Luther King, and John Lennon. The list goes on and on. You can probably think of a lot of other cases."

Now that was really spooky. Kind of crazy, even. He was saying he didn't want to be noticed because he was afraid of what might happen to him if he were.

Instead of clearing up my questions, he had given me something else to wonder about: Why had he seemed to separate himself from others? It was as though he didn't think he was human like the rest of us. That's really crazy, isn't it?

As graduation neared, Bobby and I made plans for the future. I had won a sports scholarship to State

University. Bobby was going to work in his father's video store. Andy didn't talk about the future.

Then the school's guidance counselor asked a lot of the better students if they'd like to try for state scholarships. She didn't ask Andy. But he showed up on the day of the exams and took a seat with the others.

Andy, I learned, was the first to hand in his papers and leave the room. The test takers had been allowed four hours to complete their work. Andy left after little more than an hour. Everyone thought he had given up when he found out how hard the tests were.

When the winners of the scholarships were announced, Andy's name was on the list. His score was neither the highest nor the lowest. It was somewhere in the middle.

That fall Andy and I got on the bus to State University. I was glad someone I knew was going with me. I was pleased Andy would be around. I had never been a very good student. Andy had helped me study in the past. It would be good to have his help in college.

We were pretty close that first year. Many of our classes were the same. Andy's dorm was near mine. And he did help me with my schoolwork. Andy had to maintain high grades to keep his scholarship. He couldn't keep playing the role of Mr. Average Student.

The situation changed the second year. I didn't see as much of Andy. We didn't share as many classes. And Mary had also won a scholarship. She, too, was now a student at State.

"Mary is a lot like you, isn't she?" I asked Andy one day.

He knew what I meant. Sometimes it seemed he could read my mind. "She's *exactly* like me," he said. "That's why we get along so well."

This year Andy and I share only one class—anthropology. Someone had told me it would be easy. That was important to me. When you're in school on a sports scholarship, you spend a lot of time on the practice field. Then, too, there are the games and the traveling. It really eats into study time.

Andy is in the Computer Science Department. He is studying to be a systems designer. I don't know why he took anthropology. He signed up for it after I told him I was taking the class. I was happy to see him there. It turned out to be an interesting class but a lot of work. I figured I was sure to need his help before the semester was over.

In class yesterday, the professor was talking about how much the human race has changed over the ages. We can learn about people who lived a long time ago by studying their bones. Many people were quite different from one another physically. Today only *homo sapiens,* our type of human, survives. But there have been a number of different kinds of people on the Earth.

I raised my hand. There was something I had to know. "Was there ever a time when two or more different kinds of humans shared the same area?" I asked.

"Certainly," the professor answered. "The change from one type to another didn't happen overnight. It was very gradual."

"How did the groups get along?" I asked.

"Not very well, I'm afraid. There are no records, of course, so we have no way of knowing with certainty what happened. We can make a good guess, though. There is evidence that at least one early group used another for food. Crushed skulls have been found as well as bones that had been split to expose the marrow."

The professor sat on the edge of his desk before continuing. "The first few members of any new species probably had it rough. They were surrounded by people, maybe even members of their own families or tribes, who hated them for being different. Later, when their numbers increased, the new people used cunning and greater strength to defeat their enemies. The two types had a hard time living together in peace."

I had almost forgotten Andy was in that classroom with me. I looked over at him and found him looking back. He wore an I-told-you-so expression.

By now, of course, I'm certain Andy is a new kind of human being. He has powers and abilities the rest of us don't have.

Andy also has a deathly fear of being noticed, of being singled out as different. He doesn't want the rest of the world to know what he is.

The thing I can't figure out is why he's willing to share so much of his secret with me. Although he never volunteers information, it seems to please him when I notice something no one else does.

Why doesn't he fear me the same way he fears everyone else? Is it because I've always been his friend and have proven that his secret is safe with me? Is it because I've never betrayed him?

Walking back to my room after class, I took a detour through a nearby park. A little girl was exercising a huge black dog that was nearly half-again her size. When the dog stopped running, she knelt and put her thin arms around its neck. Fearlessly, she held it while she attached a leash to its collar.

Fearlessly she held it. That powerful dog was bigger than she was. But it was her pet. She knew it too well to fear it.

Suddenly, I realized why Andy doesn't fear me. It isn't because I'm his friend. It's because he thinks of me the same way people often think of their pets. I might be dangerous, but not to him. Never to him.

When I figure out something no one else has, Andy is pleased to see me showing a bit more intelligence and insight than our classmates. To him I'm like a pet who has learned a difficult new trick. It gives him pleasure. That's why he wasn't disturbed when he heard me talking to the professor in class. Andy signed up for anthropology to be there with me. He wanted to see whether I would make the connections.

There's no other explanation I can think of.

Andy is superior—physically and mentally—to the rest of us. But two major human flaws—fear and prejudice—have been intensified, too. These flaws have been magnified to such a degree that he views anyone not like him as a threat.

People who are prejudiced never see their feelings clearly. Andy, despite his intelligence, is no different in that regard. He thinks he's being careful because ordinary people might hurt him if they knew the truth about him.

But it's Andy who is filled with hate. He feels about people the way some of us feel about snakes and spiders. He doesn't love them. He doesn't even like them. What he feels more than anything else is fear.

Andy has no real reason to think he's in danger. It's all part of his sickness. Because he hates and fears ordinary people, he's sure they would feel the same way if they knew about him.

I'm an exception. Andy knows me almost as well as I know myself. He knows what I'm proud of and what I'm ashamed of. He knows my successes and my failures. He's familiar with my hopes and my dreams. Andy doesn't fear, hate, or worry about me.

But what about his girlfriend Mary? How would she feel about me? Andy had said she's exactly like him.

If Mary is exactly like him, I imagine she has the same fears Andy has. And those fears are probably breeding hatred and distrust.

If Mary doesn't know about me already, she soon will. Andy, I'm sure, tells her everything. How will she feel about an ordinary human knowing their secret?

And what if there are others I don't know about? If there are two of them, there could be more. There could be many more, and they might be able to recognize one another as easily as Andy spotted Mary that day at Arrow Lake. If Andy and Mary tell them about me, what will the reaction be?

It scares me.

I think I'd better talk to someone about this. But who? And what will I say? Will anyone believe I know people like this? I can hardly believe it myself. How can I expect anyone else to believe it?

* * *

My name is Martin Kramer. I'm a student at State University.

This morning I found the story you just read inside a used anthropology book I bought. It had been torn from a notebook and hidden between the pages of the larger volume.

This afternoon I went to the university administration office. I learned that Hector Luz was a student here two years ago. No one knows why he left or what happened to him.

I also found out that Andrew and Mary Garrett are grad students working on their master's degrees. The couple live in a small house on a narrow side street near the university.

I walked over there this evening. The house looked much the same as all the others on the block. There wasn't a thing unusual about it.

There was a party or perhaps a meeting of some sort going on. Small groups of guests were arriving. They were all very ordinary looking. They wore no bright colors but dressed in dark tones of gray, brown, and blue. Their cars were all medium-sized gray models.

I think I was seen watching the house. I have the feeling someone followed me home.

There's the doorbell. I'll hide this before I answer it. Just in case . . .